Everything is Ephemera

poems

Dennis Etzel, Jr.

Kellogg Press   Topeka, KS

Everything is Ephemera
Copyright © 2020 Dennis Etzel, Jr.

All rights reserved. No part of this publication may be reproduced, distributed, or transmitted in any form or by any means, without prior written permission of the copyright holder.

Published by Kellogg Press
Topeka, KS
kelloggpress.com

Printed in the United States of America

Curtis Becker, Editor/Layout and Design/Cover Design
curtisbeckerbooks.com

Hailey East, Cover Art

ISBN: 978-0-578-63365-7

Table of Contents

Ars Poetica on New Year's Day	1

I   That School

A House Without Books	5
My School Inside That School	6
My Fifth-Grade Handwriting	8
My Collection with Sentimentality	9
Ars Poetica with Baseballs	10
My Clothing	11
Fascination Street	12

II   My School

At Washburn University, Topeka, Kansas	17
Walking Distances	19
Wasted Years	21
Elegy for Dr. Jorge Nobo	22
My Clutter	23
Sacred Spaces of Morgan Hall	24
Don't Stop Believing	25
Has Technology Changed the Way You Write?	26
I Have the Optimism of a Poet	27
Resistance	28
Our Union	29
Ars Poetica While Listening to Coltrane's Giant Steps While Trying to Cross 17th Street	30

III   Homeschool

At Home with the Boys as Antithesis to Writing Poetry	35
Ars Poetica with Three Year Olds	36
Homeschool Blues	37
In the New House After Our Struggles with the Old House	38
Asmund's Summer	39
Wystan as Saint Francis	40
Raedan Played with the Blinds	41
Asmund Like Orpheus	42
Raedan's Steps	43
Wystan Language	44
Runaways	45
Dad	46
An Abcedarianist Visits the Pond	47
Lessons of Summer	49
Our Movie Theatre	50
Ars Poetica with a Flooded Basement	51
Ars Poetica While Moving	52
Ars Poetica While Recycling and Thinking of William Stafford	53
Everything is Ephemera	54
Ars Poetica on New Year's Eve	59

Acknowledgements
With many thanks to the editors of these literary magazines in which poems have appeared: I-70 Review and Coal City Review

for

Margy

&

Carrie

&

the Washburn University community

purificatus non consumptus
non nobis solum

Ars Poetica on New Year's Day

playing the vinyl for the opening
high hat with electric guitar cry
piano key echoes into a human lament
even through the cold and grey
there is work to be done
each small task of what will be done
this coming year with family time
time to read time to plan the semester
time to dance to Bono's sing screams
we can break through and be one
this one is for the other years
days felt nothing felt to be the future
sleeping was the day's calling
so now I can wake a smidgen of words
so now I can work to relish the calendar
with all of its empty boxes as invitations
to make a mark in each one

I

That School

A House Without Books

I grew up in this house
many of us did
the phrase if the walls could talk
originated here
because children and walls did not
walls had no support
like you would find
in homes with bookshelves
firmly attached
no laughter
in the hallways like you might
find when opening a page
anyone's room
an entire story
in each pull from a shelf
our shelves
said nothing either I found
no entryway
into other houses
our house did not connect
but still the same
even though separate
we liked solitude
we called it a block

Dennis Etzel, Jr.

My School Inside That School

from drawing Red Five the X-Wing Fighter
fighting off the TIE Fighter teacher
who circles around me to attack
tells me to go into the hallway
to copy the dictionary
for the rest of the day
to smeared pencil-lead sheets
at the end of the day she collects
my work with pursed lips
while I leave those pages meet
the lips of the trash can
but comic books and Edith Hamilton
keep me speaking through decades
of mythological creatures like me
pursued even the minotaur
had no choice but to be himself
thrown into a prison for being himself
a labyrinth only he could knew
the way out of but feared for his life
if he ever tried to step out
feared for being shamed
so Friday nights became stories
Science Fiction and Fantasy films
on VCR carried in a pouch
alongside D&D Guides character sheets
dungeon drawings patterned from
the classroom all these saving spells

Everything is Ephemera

alongside pictures of resistance
became maps became treasures

Dennis Etzel, Jr.

My Fifth-Grade Handwriting

slouched the way the back of an L
can slant when I wrote it out
of banishment
set apart like Atlas
from the fifth-grade world
carrying the dictionary
on my back into the hallway
ostracized as a verb in a past tense
another word I found when copying pages
she did mean for words to be punishments
called a troublemaker for tracing the walls
measured the floor foot by foot
looking for trapdoors as secret escapes
but I obeyed with paper and pencil
an indention in my finger
I still feel where the pencil pushed
those smudged pages I turned over
to her grinning as she threw them away
nowadays I write by hand to reshape
hallways into exits

My Collection with Sentimentality

a wall of cardboard bricks storing baseball
cards
movie and comic book cards included
call me a boy one-hundred percent Americana
on my bicycle for the Friday trip
to the Kwik Shop when new cards stocked
seems too Rockwellian
ready to pose with my grinning face
a five-dollar quest for packaged wonder
I was a collector of pop culture
these small photos pressed onto cardboard
easy to lose value if handled carried as if mint
could be attainable the highest price for a card
never touched as if still packaged
what we Americans do with the past

Dennis Etzel, Jr.

Ars Poetica with Baseballs

on the surface
one can count
the stitchings
holds together
two parts
clasp themselves
thread windings
go unseen
until taken apart
layers surround
deeper layers
until at the core
a center
which if cracked open
falls apart
pieces as proof
that the construction
needs to stays constructed
gives this sphere flight
when thrown
by a hand
into the field

My Clothing

I wore rock shirts to roam
through concert halls in lieu
of high school Star Wars to leave
this galaxy I even sought
refuge with a Les Miz
shirt Collette within
blue red and white my
castle on a cloud over
one hundred different escape
plans filled my dresser pushed
out onto the floor each
evacuation a drape of cotton
I placed my arms
through pushed
my head into a hole
to disappear

Dennis Etzel, Jr.

Fascination Street

another day down
I'm down another day
not sick but depressed
like how that Cure song
sounds on tape played
loud enough to feel pressed
synthesizer keys while
that background hiss keeps
hissing please listen
I don't cry out
Robert Smith cries
visiting this street again
looking at river in the gutter
sinks deeper Facebook posts
do nowadays following
one self-care article down
to another could I reach out
on Facebook in the stream?
I don't want to drag you
down with me Spotify reminds me
The Cure concert tour is nowhere
near as guitars wail on reverb
Robert Smith looks as old
as I look old without makeup
I will let you know when
I'm putting on my face
I'm putting on the late Eighties
years I thought he sang put

but he sang pull on your face
I don't have a way to play
cassette tapes while the old
tapes sometimes click back on
to play inside me so I
put on my hair
put on my pout
listen give me a calms
forté to slip me over
sleep's shoulder because
I love tomorrow

II

My School

At Washburn University, Topeka, Kansas

hit by the boom fireworks
made when overhead
you feel your life split
half of your life spent
on campus
staying focused with attention
even today half-awake
on the east side of Morgan Hall
you notice for the first time
the dome
of the State Capitol Building
with all of downtown
panorama
of your whole life here
in Topeka in Kansas
center of the country
center of the city
merely existing as a student
who travelled through
buildings surrounding the campus
when Morgan's half-working tower
chimed half a bell
remember half of your mind
in a notebook
writing about the other half
in a crumby job
when a professor reaches
your hemispheres

Dennis Etzel, Jr.

    with notebook with thesaurus
    your words double
    with your classes
    you come back for English
    for the words
    run up the hill double-speed
    to make it to Henderson
    roam through the Union
    still remodeling
    what you see
    in double vision
    who you were
    who you are
    both sides as a student
    as a professor
    new buildings rise
    in your own buildings

Walking Distances

two blocks
to the university
one block I was
unable to speak
the other a need
to find words
poetry is the birth
of language
someone said
through me
I discovered
mine through this
distance
knowing the line it takes
to cast with a pen
some ground
yes I was
a student who went
years trying
until I could
so I never left
this radius
blocks switch
into stanzas
for building I am
student of conduits
I sit in
temporary offices

Dennis Etzel, Jr.

    like mentors had
    where if you come visit
    come through any open door

Wasted Years

money's still tough going without
but teaching's better than years
of bad friends bad love caught
in a corporate world I felt trapped

at McDonald's again doing dishes
the lowest low volume listening
to Iron Maiden's "Wasted Years"
as mantra against golden arches

for golden years countless
burgers thrown out after ten minutes
we sometimes stretched to fifteen
anything to feel we hadn't failed

in our calculations even years
later visiting a student at his McDonald's
my old boss Gina asked if I like teaching
as if we are still both stuck

Dennis Etzel, Jr.

    Elegy for Dr. Jorge Nobo

    you were alive when describing Spinoza
    filling the chalkboard with Spinoza
    with words with pictures with linear waves
    in the way Spinoza explained reality
    as a projection of God and we were inhabitants

    when you called me
    into your office I thought I failed
    instead you said I understood the tenets
    of our studies but wasn't a great writer
    followed with encouragement to track
    with a journal and thesaurus the way words
    move connect from book to page
    while a whisper enters to help

    Spinoza spoke there even after you erased
    the day from the board
    piercing eyes someone said about you
    while with your deep focal glasses
    you set us at ease
    like any metaphysical truth
    we felt seen

    like Whitehead you showed
    me my being is constituted by my becoming

My Clutter

piles of books and papers
from my college days
linger because I never left
they trail through
my phases of student to graduate
to colleague
with my own office
even bookshelves disappear
behind books
which is why I keep
my door shut
why this year
I am taking Marie's class
she asks
are these books beneficial
to your life
going forward?
in May I graduate

Dennis Etzel, Jr.

Sacred Spaces of Morgan Hall

the desk that you sit in I sat in years ago
in this same room we see
these desks will soon be replaced
don't let that stop you
when I was there I had the dream
of being a computer programmer
I made that dream come true
until I had to find a way to see past
my cubicle under the vents piping in
stale air with toxins I had to come back to
this desk I had to bring my journal
why I ask you to keep your journal
not simply a notebook but hardback
for poems written on acid-free pages

Don't Stop Believing

I am sick of that song too
many of my students don't believe
how can one stop if not started?
it is true I had to do
I had to write myself out of myself
I had to write myself back in
I had to write myself as another me
but I wrote nothing for a long time
I am sick of Journey
I don't want to hear the past again
I lived through those songs
I want to live through new songs
my students help with lyrics
I won't stop believing in poems
poems always believed me

Dennis Etzel, Jr.

Has Technology Changed the Way You Write?

the student asks as if wanting to hear me pro-
test
as a poet and professor the use of cellphones

as if I would only put words down with ink
like a tattoo permanent for good

I confess I hold my cell phone
alongside my pen in my pocket

so wherever I am in the middle
of words they can be captured

Facebook Messenger like Hermes transcribing
voice-to-text doing his work in the sky

I Have the Optimism of a Poet

I lead my students through the halls
to write about this college life
some feel the barriers for writing
I feel the barriers for writing
a professor tells me as a student
I need to be a better writer
keep a notebook
carry a thesaurus
I unpack my backpack
take out those broken barriers
teachers showed me how to make
mistakes I couldn't finish either
I finish a poem in typing class
click-click-click-click
A-A-A-space
click-click-click-click
A-A-A-space
I spaced out my world
so a poem came
students share their college
share within this space
even the worst of words appear
when strolling through a line
these words are the concrete
I say with the optimism of a poet
while my feet rest on broken boards
my poem for the class ending

Dennis Etzel, Jr.

Resistance

time this reserved space like Blake wrote about
eternity in an hour we try
every week to place a poem into
as our caveat of no grading no
lesson planning no students no meetings

makes this room as a stanza these other
demands won't fit into or a sonnet
where we can't measure one-fourteenth of this
sixty minutes per line if we insist
we fight the Patriarchy through teaching

we need to break the form by breaking lines
compose by recomposing an aubade
each Monday every time
changing notes to that recovered song

for Jericho

Our Union

I spend an hour in your University's Student
        Union
to write and imagine I teach here sit here in this
        chair
which becomes the plush chair in Washburn's
        Union
both bookstores close early in the summer so
        students
search alongside employees staff and us faculty
        for a space

until fall when the huge clock picks up speed to
        show
signs of our school's rivalry with yours blue
        versus gold
there will be the famous football game with can
        donations
but I'm not here to start something I'm here to
        continue
our friendship where we elect our own mascot
        the poet

for Kevin

Dennis Etzel, Jr.

Ars Poetica While Listening to Coltrane's Giant Steps While Trying to Cross 17th Street

I walk with intention
headphones on
prepare yards in advance
for crossing
my stride in time
with Coltrane's pace
ready to tap the button
like a high hat
until it flashes
ready to do my work
in between the lines
strut across the blank
but the traffic doesn't do
what I want
what it should
I put a foot out

but get snapped back
stuck still
worried I will turn back
or worse
get hit
but I breathe
clear myself
for the kind helper
that recognizes the signs
for me

to place steps forward
until complete

III

Homeschool

At Home with the Boys
as Antithesis to Writing Poetry

somewhere else
is a poem

not five wild stanzas
on the loose

throughout boundaries set
by a room

to knock over shelves
each visitor

touched by small hands
eager to find

what can be in this possible
space we read

Dennis Etzel, Jr.

Ars Poetica with Three Years Olds

like a line where one word follows another
Aldwyn jumps as Eldric follows

off the coffeetable my grandmother sat behind
for years I visited her until she passed away

twenty years ago words seldom came
as the Royals were televised our breaths held

from behind coffeetable as bandstand to drift
during cool nights watching birds in flight

suddenly perch into the lights above
even blinded as there is always a landing

Homeschool Blues

when the students grow confused
as I tell them we homeschool
I say my sons love learning
a jaw drops in asking
What does your wife do?
She's at home I say
we are now both at work
teaching another
jaw drop to ask
Does she get paid?
I worry for a moment
but an alert dings on my phone
no alarm
Carrie sent a poem by Asmund
about how a legend is
the wings that fly above
the fins that swim below
the hands that grasp onto
trees that know no end
for growth

for Carrie

Dennis Etzel, Jr.

In the New House After Our Struggles with the Old House

Aldwyn growls as the T-Rex
inside a house made of plastic plates
held by magnets

he takes care of the occupant
begins work on the roof
until a giraffe interferes

stomps the walls down
I ask if the two can be friends
as Aldwyn begins rebuilding

explains the house
is a cage
the giraffe is freeing the dinosaur

Asmund's Summer

has moved the sun higher
luckily
with your fear of ghosts
there are no shadows
until you are asleep
ghosts live
in ghost towns
I try to remind you
when you ask
the sun points
out Mike's empty yard
house
you even drew a heart for him
in February
until we reminded you he had
passed on
we did not tell you suicide
we do not know
if you know that word yet
this vocabulary built
on thin air you ask me
are ghosts real? one
night in March
now it is summer everything
is quiet Kansas heat
keeps people inside
it feels like a ghost town

Dennis Etzel, Jr.

Wystan as Saint Francis

collecting lady bugs
in his lady bug shirt and hat
in order to free our wonder
through the thick traffic
threatening like mountains
our work in constriction
removed us as pilgrims
as wanderers in wonder
of cemetery stones in argument
for how hard this neighborhood breathes
in the blue-collar past that raised
trees and catalog houses
all the wood that gets stripped
by rain and wind all danger
for the little ones we pray
for mercy for the truth
that this has something more
left to be revealed like lifted wings

Raedan Played with the Blinds

until the blinds fell
and that's how I woke up falling
my place of rest behind me
the door ahead of me
small laughter followed by language
this makes me not want to lie down
to explain I could stay in a room
with a bed with sun or moon
as I did through the dark times
when I hung blankets over blinds
when the sun couldn't come through

Dennis Etzel, Jr.

Asmund Like Orpheus

turns back
to make sure I am there behind
the steps also in darkness ahead
into the woods tonight
to understand how to go to sleep
when you ask how to go to sleep
I have to think through the forest
closing my eyes it feels impossible
just to be taken either way
by not looking or looking
through the hush of darkness

Raedan's Steps

my regret of not giving your climbing
enough attention makes that ladder
longer out of the distance between you
and your brothers in boots
you will inherit jumping
around your shared bedroom
a son should be able to live his own
life without his shirt on without
anyone else's shirt on

Dennis Etzel, Jr.

Wystan Language

chooses links to the fence I built
curious about interweavings
clasped tight I follow
these columns his world
his syntax these synonyms
with idioms as he asks
do you know what I mean
by puzzle? a bicycle
and rolls along faster
that the chain appears
to be the thing in motion
I am missing out on time
with him in reference
to when he was younger
months ago legs pushing
on the pedals further
circle the ultimate question
to answer within spokes
blurred like syllables

Runaways

Asmund said he used his imagination
then ran away with it I agreed as a poet
we find ourselves rephrasing what we say
the first said thing isn't enough sometimes
we choose to run instead of say
sometimes the poem runs away

Dennis Etzel, Jr.

Dad

Asmund yells yells yells
into screams it takes him
three times to grab
my attention when I don't
mean to block those long
a cappellas of that name
of a man I feared how can I
ask my sons to stop yelling

when they need me or not they
say they need me how can I stay
stuck within a sound so primary
it takes seconds to concentrate
on to identify what sounds
link to recognize myself

An Abcedarianist Visits the Pond

Approach
Begins
Cautious

Dares
Event

Figure
Ghosts
Haunt

Inside
Journey

Know
Long
Mouths

Netherworld
Of
Pondering

Quiet
Resistance

Subtle
Touch
Upon

Dennis Etzel, Jr.

    Vibration

    Within
    Xanadu

    Your
    Zone

    for my sons

Lessons of Summer

watching my sons take swimming lessons
if it wasn't for the sun's trauma beating down
on me if it wasn't for how the skin remembers
trauma I believe summer could be summer
instead of those months the DNA remembers
underwater days I held my breath as I was told
to roam the streets with no cars no people
around too hot outside too hot to go home

it will just take some time
in hesitations I breathe repeat it will take
this pool of memories to dive underwater
against this fear of swimming even
standing along edges for too long
without falling in

Dennis Etzel, Jr.

Our Movie Theatre

Carrie took a DVD holder
from the shelf opened
it to the flat disc made to spin
within the machine the film
was on the screen not the case
I resisted caught by each cover's
importance art and text along spines
with titles sorted and lined
like books where books could be

after placing hundreds in a folder
my relief came flooding as fast
as plastic melts for recycling
I could carry the films I love
like a portable movie theatre
now we rarely pull the two cases out
as we watch movies at night
from an ethereal cloud
on a phone held up close
in its ephemera

Ars Poetica with a Flooded Basement

sometimes the rain catches one off guard
with a wet-vac motor burning sucking up
all one can get into a barrel to realize
it fills needs dumped begin again
searching through damaged things
needing thrown out move back
forth around pulling everything up
then resurface when finished in the air
without mildew without mold through
these dry rooms protected

Dennis Etzel, Jr.

Ars Poetica While Moving

this start of a poem slips away
when I am needed in the other room
to help move a sofa a word
followed another word out the door
as one was stuck in the fresh paint
I know three poems escaped
although I don't remember what
they look like some were lost

in the move itself fell off the truck
or along the road where I left
my goodbyes others just left
in the anxiety but at the new place
they are found carried in by my sons
spring out of the opened boxes

Ars Poetica While Recycling and Thinking of William Stafford

I've rarely
found golden
threads they are
aluminum easily
breaks into parts
I store away
recycle later

Dennis Etzel, Jr.

Everything is Ephemera

taking an April
afternoon at Washburn
University Topeka
Kansas drifting
I was in the Union
basement depressed
after my first six years
not knowing if I would
take on a fierceness
of dandelions or
simply be blown
like its seeds spent
five more years
my first degree
in computers
back for a second
degree in English
to leave that world
of programming
I had the will to leap
my best triumphs
in the midst of crumbling
back then you waved
I could not wave back
but now I can
take a selfie with my smile
Washburn in the background
students stroll around

Everything is Ephemera

my colleague Jericho nods
we should move on
Kansas winds blow
our pens like cars
along 17th Street
we have somewhere to go
prospective students visit
as others pose
for graduation pictures
along this circle in front
I circled around
thanks to you
some who rejected
should see me out here
I plant myself
but the riding lawnmower
cuts it close
we search for utopia
in the grasses
your Romantic
Movement never ends
my own path twists
like a question mark
the point of this all
non consumptus
as I motto I would not be
consumed by any fire
not even my own
I can't help but visit
then check myself

Dennis Etzel, Jr.

    students get to meet you
    through me as you are
    out on the prairie
    taking care of clouds
    as they roll to me
    I catch your air like tall grass
    roots growing each year
    even the noxious weeds
    are allowed to pass me
    you know the type
    as finals come with final
    days of any semester
    never finalized
    always tumbling
    grasses make the shape
    of this tiny globe

    for Margy Stewart

Ars Poetica on New Year's Eve

be winter
be the solace
outside
be the sky's grey
to write a line upon
be the song
Auld Lang Syne
be last year
be the dropping
of the ball
in Time's Square
be the light
that reflects
into hundreds
of beams
be the crowd
be the candle's
constant
promise of fire

About the Author

Dennis Etzel Jr. lives with Carrie and the boys in Topeka, Kansas where he teaches English at Washburn University. His work has appeared in Denver Quarterly, Indiana Review, BlazeVOX, Fact-Simile, 1913: a journal of poetic forms, 3:AM, Tarpaulin Sky, DIAGRAM, and others. He is a recipient of The Kansas City Star Best Poetry Book selection in 2015, a 2017 Kansas Notables Book selected by the State of Kansas Library, a 2017 Troy Scroggins Award, and the 2017 Topeka ARTSConnect Arty Award in Literary Arts. He leads poetry workshops in various Kansas spaces.

Praise for Everything is Ephemera

Everything is Ephemera is a collection of introspections catalogued by time and place I'd file under 'must-read' for any student or teacher of poetry and parent alike. Dennis reminds me that the phases of student to teacher to colleague are cyclical and don't only occur in academia.

    -Huascar Medina, Poet Laureate of Kansas (2019-2021), Un Mango Grows In Kansas

Everything Is Ephemera is a book about education, in three parts—childhood, college, fatherhood. Dennis Etzel, Jr., understands that who you were is also who you are. He is still the boy copying dictionary words for a teacher who meant "for words to be punishments." These poems have no periods, no borders. He has traded his dictionary for a thesaurus, and he writes to "reshape hallways into exits." Everything is ephemera, true; moments and poems slip from our grasp. But the collection of moments becomes a whole life, and words from forgotten poems find their way into new ones, which find their way into unforgettable collections like this one.

    -Melissa Fite Johnson, A Crooked Door Cut into the Sky

In one poem the fifth-grade teacher orders her student into the hall to copy pages from the dictionary, "words…punishments," but Etzel turns words into joy, into magic, into redemption through these poems, these pages, which include meditations on a childhood of science fiction movies, Dungeons & Dragons, comic books, and the kind of quiet observation and reflection that lead to early wisdom.

    -Kevin Rabas, Poet Laureate of Kansas, 2017-2019, Watch Your Head

Also Available from Kellogg Press

Vacant Childhood
Lindsey Bartlett

He Watched and Took Note
Curtis Becker

Six Feet Apart
AJ Dome

Dirt Road
Kerry Moyer

Rust & Weeds
Kerry Moyer

I Love the Child
Ronda Miller

Winds of Time
Ronda Miller

Watch Your Head
Kevin Rabas

Watch Your Head 2
Kevin Rabas

Order online at kelloggpress.com

www.ingramcontent.com/pod-product-compliance
Lightning Source LLC
Chambersburg PA
CBHW021413290426
44108CB00010B/508